185 TIPS ON
WORLD
BUILDING

FROM
THE ART OF WORLD BUILDING
SERIES

RANDY ELLEFSON

Evermore Press
GAITHERSBURG, MARYLAND

Evermore Press, LLC
Gaithersburg, Maryland
www.evermorepress.org

185 Tips on World Building / Randy Ellefson. -- 1st ed.
ISBN 978-1-946995-35-3 (Amazon paperback)
ISBN 978-1-946995-33-9 (IngramSpark paperback)

CONTENTS

ACKNOWLEDGEMENTS

Edited by JJ Henke

Cover design by Randy Ellefson

INTRODUCTION

Subscribers to *The Art of World Building* newsletter receive tips in their inbox. These tips are collected here in this short volume and organized by the books from which they came.

ABOUT ME

By profession I'm a software developer, but I've been writing fantasy fiction since 1988 and building worlds just as long, mostly one planet called Llurien. Yes, I am crazy. But I love what I do. I didn't intend to work on it for so long, but when life has prevented me from writing, I've worked on Llurien. I've done everything in these chapters and authored two hundred thousand words of world building in my files. Llurien even has its own website now at http://www.llurien.com.

I've written several novels and more than a dozen short stories over the years, and began my publishing career with a novella that you can read for free (see below). Also a musician with a degree in classical guitar, I've released instrumental rock albums, a classical guitar CD, and a disc of acoustic guitar instrumentals. You can learn more, hear songs, and see videos at my main website, http://www.randyellefson.com.

FREE BOOK

If you'd like to see a free sample of my own world building efforts in action, anyone who joins my fiction newsletter mailing list receives an eBook of *The Ever Fiend (Talon Stormbringer)*. Please note there's a separate newsletter for *The Art of World Building*, though both can be joined on the same signup form. Just check the box for each.

TEMPLATES AND NEWSLETTER

Effective world building requires having written down details about the created world. To help you organize and jumpstart your efforts, each volume in this series includes templates in the appendices. While these templates are not included in this book, you can download these templates for free by joining the newsletter for *The Art of World Building*. As each volume is published, whether you've bought the book or not, subscribers will automatically receive an email with links to download the templates as Microsoft Word files, which you can repeatedly use. Visit http://www.artofworldbuilding.com/newsletter/.

WORLD BUILDING UNIVERSITY

World Building University (WBU) has online courses that provide step-by-step instruction on how to create all aspects of great fantasy and science fiction worlds. Each includes a series of video lessons, quizzes to test your retention of what you've learned, and assignments designed to make your creation a reality instead of a dream. Courses are intended for both authors, game designers, and hobbyists. A free course is available to get you started! See the website or mailing list for details:

http://www.worldbuilding.university/

THE PODCAST

The Art of World Building podcast expands on the material within the series. The additional examples offer world builders more insight into ramifications of decisions. You can hear the podcast, read transcripts, and learn more about the episodes.

http://www.artofworldbuilding.com/podcasts.

CHAPTER ONE

CREATING LIFE TIPS

Everything we need to know about how to create gods, species/races, plants, animals, monsters, heroes, villains, and even undead is included in *Creating Life (The Art of World Building, #1)*. Some basic techniques are also discussed, such as using analogies and deciding how many worlds to build in a career. As with every volume, this book includes reusable templates that can help you build better, faster.

The tips in this section are from *Creating Life (The Art of World Building, #1)*.

ANALOGUES

These tips come from Chapter 1.

TIP #1: USE ANALOGUES

An analogue is a world-building element that has a corresponding version on Earth. Maybe we create a country modeled on Japan, using cultural and physical elements so that we don't have to invent everything from scratch. This shortcut helps us create realistic items for our world but has a caveat of being less interesting and less original. Use wisely and you can save time and effort.

TIP #2: THE RULE OF THREE

It's more of a guideline than a rule, but when using an analogue, it's a good idea to make at least three major changes to it so our audience doesn't immediately recognize it. A large, four-legged, pack animal with big tusks, floppy ears, and a trunk is obviously an elephant. What would you change to make it seem new?

TIP #3: DON'T USE NAMES POORLY

Avoid using a familiar name for something that's very different from something on Earth. If you call something an elf, people expect pointed ears. Failure to follow certain expectations will make them assume you don't know what you're doing. Use a new name if you've changed anything fundamental.

TIP #4: MIX AND MATCH ANALOGUES

We can combine elements from different analogues to help obscure where we got the idea. Take staple foods from one land (like rice and fish from Japan), culture from another (like Nazi Germany), and the typical appearance (including clothing) of people from a third (an African tribe). Look at Earth like a buffet from which you can create a unique meal.

TIP #5: MAKE IT WORTH IT

Audiences have short memories, so we should keep an analogue easy to describe and remember. This is aided by making the changes significant. Adding two extra legs to a horse may not be worth it, especially if all the horses are that way. It's not like the six-legged kind are faster than the four-legged ones that don't exist in your world. Make the alterations relevant or leave it like the original.

HOW MANY WORLDS

The following tips come from Chapter 1 of *Creating Life*.

TIP #1: DETERMINE YOUR GOALS

If you're planning a long career, it may make sense to build one world extensively. Otherwise you might build 20 worlds for 20 books. Is that more or less work than one in-depth setting? Figure out your intentions.

TIP #2: USE EXTREME WORLDS SPARINGLY

Extreme worlds might best be suited to one-off stories due to the risks inherent in taking big chances with believability. Such places are ideal for SF when characters are planet-hopping. But there's no reason characters in a fantasy setting can't be using magic or portals to do the same thing.

Tip #3: Be Earth-like Most Often

For any setting that's frequently used, it's wise to make it Earth-like in many basic respects (gravity, light, oxygen, etc.) unless we intend to show the unusual features often. If we're less into world building, this is the default approach. We can change a few things, like adding species similar to dwarves, elves, and dragons, while keeping the rest familiar to our readers.

Tip #4: Reclaim Wasted Time

World building can be done in small bits. We don't need to devote months on end like with a novel, where we can lose our train of thought if we stop. It's a great way to reclaim lost time, like when standing in line somewhere - jot down ideas on your phone and flesh them out later. College often prevented me from writing, so I did world building in small bits, ten or thirty minutes at a time when I felt like it or had an idea.

Tip #5: Don't Get Overwhelmed

Remember that world building is optional. Yes, we might need to create a setting, but we can essentially make it Earth by another name if desired. Don't let world building become a chore or get overwhelmed by a big to-do list. Otherwise, you'll just give up. World building is fun!

SUMMARY OF CHAPTER 1—
WHY BUILD A WORLD?

While world building is expected in many genres of fantasy and SF, we must decide how many worlds to build. This will depend on our career plans and goals. Learn the advantages and disadvantages of building one world for each story vs. one world for many stories, and when to take each approach. Sometimes doing both is best, allowing for greater depth in one world but the option to step away to keep things fresh. Using analogues can help us create believable societies quickly but has pitfalls that can be avoided. Do you have the ability to create many interesting worlds, and will they have enough depth to make the effort worth it?

THE GODS

These tips come from Chapter 2 of from *Creating Life*.

TIP #1: DECIDE WHETHER TO CREATE THEM

A story that doesn't need gods frees us from inventing them. That might change if the setting is a world we'll use often, as a religious character would crop up sooner or later. But single-use worlds can get away without deities, though it's arguably better to just create a lone god and skimp on details or a pantheon. If you don't have a feel for what to do, skip this...or read *Creating Life* to gain ideas.

TIP #2: SCIENCE DOESN'T ELIMINATE RELIGION

A popular theory states that with more science we have less religion, but look at our own world to see how much religion exists despite all our scientific accomplishments. Science may explain things that were once held to be of divine origin, but beliefs persist. Your world's inhabitants will still believe in a higher being, most likely, even if you decide not to comment on it.

TIP #3: ARE THE GODS REAL?

In fantasy, deities are typically real and sometimes appear. SF often doesn't mention the gods, but if so, they seldom show up. Decide if the world's gods are real and whether they interfere in events. What are some famous incidents and consequences? Read *Creating Life* for ideas.

TIP #4: WE CAN REUSE DEITIES

If we create a detailed setting we repeatedly use, gods are one of the subjects we need to invent only once because they exist outside the scope of our current story and can be reused. This is one reason to create a single well-developed world. One detailed pantheon can be more entertaining and be a common theme across stories. Why create pantheons over and over?

TIP #5: USE ANALOGUES

We can borrow gods of various Earth pantheons and alter them to fit our setting. This helps us get started. At the least, we can create a list of gods and their attributes and then start mixing and matching what we like to create our versions, like Dr. Frankenstein creating gods.

TIP #6: CREATE A PANTHEON

A group of gods is more work to invent but offers opportunities for conflicts among the deities. These can reflect cultural and moral issues, such as myths about gods facing struggles similar to those of their worshipers. Pantheons offer a good way to characterize our residents, as everyone might worship someone else.

TIP #7: MAKE THE GODS VULNERABLE

Beings that can't be hurt or killed are less interesting. If you decide one is dead or wounded, determine how, who did it, and the impact on gods and mortals alike. Do they die from natural causes, too? For ideas, read *Creating Life.*

TIP #8: CHILDREN

Make your gods capable of reproducing, whether that creates more gods, demi-gods, or just super humans (or other species). This can give a world heroes like Hercules. It can even make a mortal woman want to seduce a god. Now there's a story idea!

TIP #9: HOW DOES TIME END?

Decide how life as everyone knows it will end, even if you never use this in a story beyond someone mentioning your world's Armageddon. It's fun deciding how everyone will be destroyed. Find a good reason for it happening, whether it's moral decay or something more physical.

TIP #10: CREATE MYTHS

Myths make a world more entertaining, but only invent them if there's a chance they'll be used. Self-publishers can use a myth as bonus materials in a newsletter, website, or short story.

SUMMARY OF CHAPTER 2—GODS

Our species will invent gods to believe in even if we don't invent them, so we may need some deities for people to reference in dialogue, whether praying or swearing. In SF, belief in gods may still exist despite, or even because of, advances in science. In fantasy, priests often call on a god to heal someone, and this requires having invented the gods. Pantheons offer advantages over a lone god, including dynamic relationships between them and the species. Half gods and demigods are other options that help us create myths and legends to enrich our world, especially if gods can be born, die, or be visited in their realm.

SPECIES

These tips come from Chapter 3 of from *Creating Life*.

TIP #1: DECIDE WHETHER TO CREATE THEM

Some SF and even fantasy (like *Game of Thrones*) has nothing but humans, so you may not need to invent a species at all. Or you might be writing a genre with public domain races you can use, like elves. We can do a mix of these, using the latter while inventing a few of our own, but this has risks, too. Read *Creating Life* to understand why and how to manage them. The best reason to invent is arguably that you have a great idea.

TIP #2: DECIDE IF THEY'RE SPECIES OR RACES

We have leeway to call our humanoids species or race, but it might be best to use both terms and create a hierarchy that makes it easier to understand relationships. Decide which ones inherited DNA from others or which ones developed on their own, or were independently created by the gods. This is fundamental to creating relationships. Volume 1 explains how to structure humanoids for the best of both worlds.

TIP #3: DETERMINE HOW YOU'LL USE THEM

A race that's just a monster in the woods is easier to create than one that must have a full culture and stand alongside classic races as a well-developed humanoid. Consider how your invention can be used to discover benefits and limitations that you can either accept or overcome. Maybe the "monster in the woods" version isn't allowed in cities, so you create a tamer race that is accepted; this can cause complexity, realism, and fun plot points as characters aren't sure which they're dealing with until too late.

TIP #4: HOW INTEGRATED ARE THEY?

A species that keeps to itself in mountains or forests will have different attitudes about others than one that gets around. Is it realistic that they're so isolated? Invent a good reason if so, such as troubling history with others. Consider having them frequently live among humans and others, as this can create even more conflict than hiding away. A tension is where stories lie.

TIP #5: DETERMINE HOW ENVIRONMENT AFFECTED THEM

Like dwarves, anything living underground is bound to be short. A forest dwelling species might not run well, while one on the plains likely does. Physical adaptations are probable unless the race lives in a wide range of environments, like us. Once this is decided, we can determine how that environment affected their culture, too. Giving thought to this makes our species more cohesive.

TIP #6: DON'T GIVE A SPECIES A UNIFORM DISPOSITION

Much of the tension in life, at least among us humans, is not knowing whether someone is good or evil, to be simplistic about it. Making invented species be uniformly one way or another makes them predictable, which is less interesting, but if we invent multiple races of them, this variety makes them more entertaining.

TIP #7: USE AVATAR CREATORS TO INVENT A HEAD

A free, online avatar creator can help you invent faces that are typical of your invented species. This can help visualize something and be provided to an artist if we want someone to draw our creation. It also helps us avoid being unintentionally ridiculous.

TIP #8: CREATE RACES FOR VARIETY

If all the elves, for example, look the same, that means a wood elf and drow can masquerade as each other. This gives us opportunities for mayhem that don't exist if every race of a species looks different. Besides, why not surprise other characters and readers alike?

TIP #9: DECIDE HOW THEY GET ALONG WITH EVERYONE, NOT JUST HUMANS

It's easy to overlook how two invented species get along with each other because we're trying to figure out how each gets along with humans. More thought given to this makes our world more believable and engaging. Envision each race's viewpoint on how people should behave and then what they think of another race's behavior.

TIP #10: DETERMINE THEIR VIEW OF MAGIC/TECHNOLOGY

We should decide how educated a species is, as this may impact their ability to do magic or invent/use technology. If they can't read and spells are hard to learn orally, they may be unable to cast them, unless they can do it without a spell, like a god. However, even uneducated species can steal a space ship, for example, and those need janitors, too, so be clever in finding ways that the less fortunate can have power that maybe they shouldn't!

SUMMARY OF CHAPTER 3—SPECIES

Audiences are familiar with using "race" to distinguish between humanoids, especially in fantasy, but species may be a more appropriate term. This chapter explores the meaning and implications of both words, with some examples of which one to use, when, and why.

Creating a species is challenging and time consuming, but the risks and rewards can be navigated and achieved, respectively. This chapter helps us decide on our goals and if the effort is worth it. SF writers might have little choice but to create species because there are no public domain species available like the elves, dwarves, and dragons of fantasy. The benefits of creating something different can outweigh the investment and help our work stand out.

An invented species must compete with legendary ones like elves, dwarves, and dragons; this chapter helps us achieve this. Starting with habitat helps us decide on physical adaptations that affect their minds, outlook, and society, and what a typical settlement might be like and even whether they live in jointly formed settlements. Their disposition affects their relationships with other species but can also limit their usefulness to us unless steps are taken to avoid this. Characteristics like intelligence, wisdom, and dexterity all play a role in how they can be used in our work, as does their society and world view, both affected by a history we can invent to integrate them with our world. Their familiarity with the supernatural and technology influences their prominence and how they compare to other life in our world.

WORLD FIGURES

These tips come from Chapter 4 of from *Creating Life.*

TIP #1: DECIDE WHO THE HEROES AND VILLAINS ARE

There are many types of world figures, some hated, others revered. In your world, what kind of people make good figures to reference? Warriors, explorers, inventors, and leaders come to mind. Determine what they did and what they're famous for by deciding how you're going to use them. As characters? Someone to mention?

TIP #2: DETERMINE THEIR STATUS

Living figures provide ongoing opportunities for new fame, but dead heroes are more revered. If they're alive, decide what they're doing now. Retired? In hiding? Imprisoned?

TIP #3: WHAT ITEMS DID THEY HAVE?

Whether the figure is alive or dead, they might've had cool items, including ships or steeds, that are lost or in the wrong hands. This is a great way to make these figures still relevant if current characters have their weapons and armor, for example. Invent some items and reasons they're famous. What can they do that others can't?

TIP #4: WHO WERE/ARE THEIR RELATIVES?

So often, the relatives of world figures aren't mentioned at all, as if everyone was born in a test tube and raised by no one. Determine who their relatives are, including descendants, and how they feel about this figure. Don't forget that every species probably has a different opinion on this guy, too; he might be a villain to one and a hero to another.

TIP #5: WHERE DID THEY LEARN?

Most famous people have special skills. Where did this guy get his? This can be important if he was a villain who killed his master for knowledge, for example. A hero might've inherited knowledge from a mentor grooming him for great things. These aspects characterize our figure and make them "human."

SUMMARY OF CHAPTER 4—WORLD FIGURES

Villains, heroes, and more give our characters admired or despised individuals who've shaped their world and inspired them. Using Earth analogues can speed the invention of such world figures, though it's best to change some details to obfuscate the similarities. Living figures can provide ongoing usefulness but the deceased can cast a long shadow, too. Their possessions can be just as famous and offer opportunities for our characters to find something helpful or dangerous. Family, friends, and enemies also provide ongoing possibilities for their life to impact our current characters.

MONSTERS

These tips come from Chapter 5 of from *Creating Life*.

TIP #1: DO YOU NEED MONSTERS?

Our story might not need monsters, but in games, what else is there to kill but species and animals? Adventuring characters need threats to worry about, but a species/animal can suffice. The best reason to invent a monster is the reason they've historically been created: to instruct us in morality and other concerns about how to live. Find your theme and invent your monster.

TIP #2: DETERMINE WHAT IT CAN DO

A monster's skills are often the reason it's terrifying. Decide on one or two traits it uses to kill, hide, or terrify people (even if on accident). This should coincide with your purpose. Get started by fantasizing scenes of people hunting it, being hunted, or fighting it, and what signs of its existence it leaves behind.

TIP #3: UNDERSTAND THE DIFFERENCE BETWEEN MONSTERS, SPECIES, AND ANIMALS

Members of a species are a lot smarter than a monster, usually, a villain like Dracula being an exception, partly because he was once human and not dead for long. Animals differ in being numerous, whereas a monster is typically the only one of its kind. But we can break these "rules" once we think about them.

TIP #4: DECIDE WHERE YOUR MONSTER ORIGINATED

Accidents are an easy way to create monsters, especially in SF, where imaginary technology can wreak havoc. But magic and other supernatural forces can do the same. Consider whether someone created your monster on purpose, too, and for what reason? This can give us a world figure. Evolution might also have led to this creature's existence. Determine its origins to create a well-formed monster.

TIP #5: DECIDE WHAT THE MONSTER WANTS

Whether it's food, revenge, security, peace and quiet, or to hoard treasure, knowing what the monster wants will determine its behavior and lair. Treasure is a silly thing for a monster to desire, given that money is only useful when we're part of society, and a monster isn't, by definition.

SUMMARY OF CHAPTER 5—MONSTERS

The difference between monsters, species, and animals is largely sophistication and numbers. Many monsters are created by accidents that transform an existing species or animal, but sometimes monsters are created on purpose. In the latter case it's especially important to decide who caused this, and why. A monster's habitat has an impact on its usefulness and sets the stage for creating atmosphere and characterization that will largely define our audience's experience with it before the terrifying reveal. Its motivation in life, or in our work, also determines what it does and the sort of trouble it's causing for our species.

PLANTS AND ANIMALS

These tips come from Chapter 6 of from *Creating Life*.

TIP #1: DECIDE WHETHER TO INVENT PLANTS OR ANIMALS

Learn the benefit of creating either and how to speed up the process using analogues or the templates from Creating Life. In SF, we really need to invent them if characters are on other worlds where plants and animals *will* be different. Fantasy can get away with mostly Earth-like life with some additions if we have ideas. *Creating Life* can help you think of some.

TIP #2: HOW WILL YOU AND CHARACTERS USE IT?

There's no reason to invent something if we don't have a plan for it. Both plants and animals are good for products to make life better. Create a list of these uses, such as decoration, food, medicine, entertainment, guards, pets, transportation, and food. This will create goals for you to achieve with invention.

Tip #3: Research Earth Analogues

Creating plants and animals from scratch isn't easy, so learn to model them on analogues from Earth. Researching even familiar ones can turn up surprising facts we didn't know. These can be used as inspiration while freeing us to tweak details to our liking. That way, we don't have to "get it right" because we're the authority.

Tip #4: Understand Classifications

Animals are classified as amphibians, birds, fish, mammals, and reptiles, while plants are classified as seedless, seeding, and flowering. Understanding the differences can help us be specific and invent details that make our new life forms worth the time it took to create them.

Tip #5: Know Your Limits

It's usually best to imagine only a few plants and animals for a setting simply because we won't have much occasion to mention them. This is true of even worlds we'll use for decades in a long career. In such cases, new life can often be invented on the fly, so this is an area of world building that is ripe for doing piecemeal rather than all at once.

Summary of Chapter 6—Plants and Animals

In fantasy, creating plants and animals is optional due to expectations that the world is very Earth-like, but in SF that takes place off Earth, audiences are more likely to expect new ones. It takes less time to create these than other life, but we'll want to consider our time investment, how often our setting will be used, whether our creations impact our work and the impression it creates, and whether the desire to do something unique and new is worthwhile for both us and our audience.

Plants and animals are classified into categories, such as cycads, conifers, and flowering plants, and amphibians, birds, fish, mammals, and reptiles. The lifecycle of the former and the behavior of the latter help distinguish them and can be used to propel or inhibit stories involving them. While we may have purposes for them as an author, our world's inhabitants have them, too, such as decoration and medicinal uses for plants, and domestication, sports, guards, pets and transportation for animals. Both can be used for food and materials to enrich life and our world.

UNDEAD

These tips come from Chapter 7 of from *Creating Life.*

TIP #1: DECIDE IF YOU NEED TO INVENT UNDEAD

Creating new undead is challenging because so many useful types are public domain, meaning we can use them without violating copyright laws. Inventing something similar to an Earth analogue is ripe for ridicule as "just a vampire with insert-minor-difference-here," for example. Make sure you really need your undead's skills, appearance, traits, or behaviors before creating them.

TIP #2: DETERMINE WHAT THE UNDEAD WANTS

Everyone needs a goal in life, or in this case, undead life. But some undead are in denial about their status, so decide if it knows it's dead and how it feels about that, or why it's unaware. This can determine whether it wants peace, revenge, or has unfinished business that keeps it here.

TIP #3: WHAT TYPE OF UNDEAD IS IT?

Determine whether an undead is non-corporeal or if it has a body, and what state of decay that body is in. That will help determine the impact it has on those who encounter it. Don't be afraid to create undead plants and animals. If it's alive, it can be dead. And if it can die, it can return.

TIP #4: DECIDE ITS ORIGINS

Did someone create your undead on purpose or by accident? We can use phenomena, technology, or magic to do this. Also decide if the undead can create more of itself, such as vampires do. This will determine their numbers, which in turn decides how much experience people have with it. That will decide if they know how to kill it.

TIP #5: CAN IT BE KILLED?

Whether or not the undead can be permanently destroyed is what the living will most want to know about it, so decide. Then figure out how and when this can be done. Feel free to be inventive, as everyone loves a good death,

SUMMARY OF CHAPTER 7—UNDEAD

Many types of undead already exist and are public domain, and it's challenging to invent something new. Undead are often classified by appearance and behavior, but it is also their origins and how they can be destroyed that will help distinguish our undead from pre-existing types. The two basic ones are those with a body, like zombies, and those without, like ghosts. Those with a body might have a soul or not. We can decide on the mental faculties of our undead by deciding if the mind goes with the soul, but there are other factors that can impair the minds and even emotional states of undead. All these affect behavior, as do their origins, goals, and what they're capable of.

CHAPTER TWO

CREATING PLACES TIPS

The life we create needs to originate from somewhere on a planet: an ocean, a continent, in a land feature (like a forest or mountain range), in a kingdom, or in a settlement. *Creating Places (The Art of World Building, #2)* goes into detail about inventing such locations and figuring out how long it takes to travel between them by various forms of locomotion: foot, horse, wagon, dragon, wooden ship, spaceship, and more. The overall rules of our world are also considered, along with inventing time, history, various places of interest, and how to draw maps. We can start our work with any one of those subjects and criss-cross between places and life, for one often impacts the other.

The tips in this section are from *Creating Places (The Art of World Building, #2)*.

PLANETS

These tips come from Chapter 2.

TIP #1: UNDERSTAND WHAT OUR MOON CAUSES

If we want a world with no moon or more than one, we should understand how this affects tides, seasons, hours in the day, and moonlight. Tidal locking is also what keeps the same side of our moon facing us, but does your moon rotate, and how quickly? And what does this imply about your worlds? More than one moon means more interesting conjunctions of planetary bodies and eclipses, too; *Creating Places* includes a spreadsheet to help determine orbits.

TIP #2: DETERMINE THE SOLAR SYSTEM'S OTHER PLANETS

There's a tendency in fantasy to not mention other planets, even though they could be seen from Earth during ancient times, not just with modern technology. In SF, world builders often decide these matters. We'll need to understand the different planet types and where they are likely to form or be now (it can change!). Mentioning them and having characters imagine that they are realms to which one can be banished, for example, adds realism.

TIP #3: BE CAREFUL WITH CONSTELLATIONS

Did you know that people in the northern hemisphere see one set of constellations and those in the south see different ones? This can matter if we decide that the world's gods have constellations. Each deity might need two of them: one for each hemisphere. Otherwise, half the world may never know they've got one, not to mention see it.

Tip #4: Don't Forget Dark Constellations

There are dark constellations that most of us in the northern hemisphere might be unaware of, because most are only visible in the southern hemisphere. These are clouds of interstellar gas that block the light of stars behind them from reaching us. These could be used to represent our "evil" deities.

Tip #5: Use Tidal Locking

The phrase "tidal locking" makes us think of tides, but it's unrelated. This means that an orbiting satellite doesn't rotate, like our Moon, which is tidally locked to Earth. This is why we always see the same side of it. This is the eventual result of all orbiting bodies, due to gravitational effects. We can use this for habitable moons. Or even a planet, which, if tidally locked to its sun, will roast on one side and freeze on the other. While this might make Earthlike life impossible, it's an interesting place to visit if properly protected.

Tip #6: Understand the Ocean's Impact

Ocean currents move in certain patterns that mean one side of a continent has warmer water than the other. This is usually the same across a world. Why does it matter? It affects what sea life might be there and what the climate is like. We don't need to leverage this, but the knowledge helps makes one location on our world feel different from another, rather than all getting no comment on the climate or its impact on vegetation, livestock, and culture.

TIP #7: USE PREVAILING WINDS TO SHAPE THE LAND

If your planet spins, it has prevailing winds, which are either east or west. Which direction depends on which way the planet rotates, but it also depends on how far from the equator we're talking. It changes direction depending on latitude and it's important to know where this happens on your continent because it affects vegetation.

TIP #8: UNDERSTAND RAIN SHADOWS

If there's a north-to-south mountain range, moisture-carrying, prevailing winds must go over them. This causes the rain to fall on the windward side of those mountains, but then there's no water left for the leeward side. The result? A desert.

TIP #9: KNOW YOUR DESERT TYPES

Hot deserts have clear, sunny skies (hence the heat) but get cold at night due to those same skies. Cold deserts are also hot during the day but brutally cold, far below freezing, in winter. Mild deserts are, well, milder than both. Each is found in certain climates or locations (inland, coastal, or at high elevations). Knowing which is found where is not only more accurate but also lets us create easily distinguishable regions.

TIP #10: USE ANALOGUES FOR CLIMATE

It can be easier to base a whole continent's climates based on a familiar region. If you know the climate in Europe, assume your continent is similar and is surrounded by similar land masses. The shapes you draw on a map can be different, but this is a quick way to get it "right" without the research!

SUMMARY OF CHAPTER 2—PLANETS

This chapter focuses on creating an Earth-like planet. World builders should understand the role of the moon and its effects on tides, seasons, and more if we intend to have a moon different from our own or multiple moons. Mention of other planets, constellations, and comets can make our world seem like it's not an island. The equator, climate zones, prevailing winds, and rain shadows all affect how much precipitation falls in an area, which in turn affects all life there, including vegetation or the lack thereof. Understanding these basics will help us create believable landscapes.

CONTINENTS

These tips come from Chapter 3 of *Creating Places*.

Tip #1: Decide How Many Continents to Create

Even if our story only takes places on one land mass, we should at least roughly create other continents and give them names. Knowing their direction from our main one and how hard they are to reach tells us and readers how likely visitors from far off lands are. Each continent might be known for a few things, such as slavery, rare gems or other items, strange regions, or interesting creatures. Some of these things might find their way to our main continent, which is why we ought to have some idea on this. It makes our continent seem less isolated.

Tip #2: Decide on the Hemisphere

If we've lived our life in one hemisphere, we might need to remind ourselves that the seasons are reversed in the other one. The visible constellations are, too, and the moon appears upside down. Most importantly, an expression like "going south for the winter" makes no sense in the southern hemisphere.

Tip #3: Understand Plate Tectonics and Mountain Ranges

We don't need to be experts in plate tectonics. Just know that explosive, volcanic mountain ranges along coastlines are common due to two plates converging there. If this happens at sea, we can find a chain of islands. But when it happens between two continental plates, we get the tallest mountains, none volcanic. But technically a volcano can happen anywhere if there's a flaw in the plate below.

TIP #4: WATERWAYS

Did you know a sea and ocean are the same thing? Sea is just used to denote a smaller area of an ocean. Bays, gulfs, coves, and fjords are all bays but of different sizes and configurations. They can be connected by a strait, channel, pass, or passage, which are also all the same thing!

TIP #5: WHAT'S AN ISLAND?

Some islands are so big that we might be tempted to call them a continent (Australia, anyone?). The distinction is largely one of size. Use your judgement. However, actual islands are either oceanic or continental. The former are far out to sea and volcanic.

SUMMARY OF CHAPTER 3—CONTINENTS

Which hemisphere our continent lies in affects the seasons and might impact where we place constellations. Understanding plate tectonics can help us build believable mountain ranges and place volcanoes where they might occur. This can also determine where deep areas of the sea are, giving our sea monsters somewhere to call home. We have some liberty in which term we use for a body of water, but this chapter includes details on when to use which name, including seas, bays, inlets, and more.

LAND FEATURES

These tips come from Chapter 4 of *Creating Places*.

TIP #1: KNOW WHERE VOLCANIC MOUNTAINS AREN'T

When an oceanic and a continental tectonic plate meet, the former descends under the latter and causes volcanoes, but when two continental plates meet, they fold on top of each other, creating the highest mountains on Earth. They also aren't volcanic. Your interior mountains will be the tallest.

TIP #2: OLYMPUS MONS ON MARS IS HUGE…AND BORING

With Mount Everest being 29,035 feet, Olympus Mons on Mars might sound far more impressive at 69,459, but it's not. It's so wide, the size of France, that you wouldn't even realize you're standing on one. It won't cut a majestic figure against the sky. Bigger isn't always better.

TIP #3: A VOLCANO CAN BE ANYWHERE

Due to random faults that appear in tectonic plates, we can put a volcano anywhere we want.

TIP #4: MOUNTAINS 'HUMANIZE' DRAGONS

Dragons often appear invincible, but if we want to be more realistic, make it harder for them to fly at high altitudes. This happens with real Earth birds, who struggle to get over very tall mountains. Making your dragons struggle, too, gives them a vulnerability and makes them seem more plausible.

TIP #5: DECIDE HOW OLD A RIVER IS

Not all rivers are alike. Younger rivers tend toward being fast, rapid, and somewhat straight. By contrast, ancient rivers are slow, wide, and meander in a zig-zig pattern.

TIP #6: KNOW YOUR FOREST TYPES

Why have every forest be a generic one when we can distinguish between forests, savannahs, woodlands, and jungles? Each gives a different impression and causes variation in animals and creatures present, plus travel conditions.

TIP #7: KNOW WHERE GRASSLANDS ARE

They tend to be located farther from a mountain range that is causing a rain shadow. It's reasonable to have a forest on one side of the mountains and a desert on the other.

TIP #8: DON'T FORGET WETLANDS!

Mires, bogs, swamps, and marshes may appear similar to us if we haven't done our research, but *Creating Places* gives you enough detail to tell and show your audience the difference. They can form boundaries that average people don't want to enter, or places from which strange creatures emerge. They also let us create a more varied landscape.

TIP #9: DESERTS TEND TO BE ROCKY

We associate sand dunes with deserts, but the majority are covered in hard, packed earth, almost like pavement. This is hard on the feet (or hooves) but offers a very different experience than sand as far as trudging along is concerned. Understand where this happens to utilize it effectively.

TIP #10: "DECIDE ON THE CULTIVATION LEVEL

Some worlds have been terraformed; others are wild, untamed expanses. Decide how much species have cultivated the world. This can include burning down forests, dumping toxic wastes, turning deserts into cities, and much more.

SUMMARY OF CHAPTER 4—LAND FEATURES

A continent will have mountains, volcanoes, lakes, rivers, forests, woodlands, savannahs, jungles, prairies, wetlands, and deserts, but world builders should understand each to place them in believable locations. While some aspects are obvious, minor details can change our decisions and augment our resulting stories. Why say characters have entered a run-of-the-mill forest when we can say it's a savannah instead, describing how it looks and what life is like for inhabitants and those traversing it? This chapter aids world builders in making a more varied landscape— one that is accurately depicted.

SOVEREIGN POWERS

These tips come from Chapter 5 of *Creating Places*.

TIP #1: IS THE SOVEREIGN RECOGNIZED?

Just because your sovereign power declares itself one, that doesn't mean other countries acknowledge this sovereignty. Even within a power, some might not recognize it. This sort of dispute gives rise to stories like *Game of Thrones*. When Napoleon dubbed himself emperor of France, the rest of Europe disagreed. We can leverage such scenarios.

TIP #2: YOU'RE HEAD OF WHAT?

There's a difference between the head of state and head of government, though the same person can be both. Certain government types separate them while others don't. Conflict can be achieved by pitting two people against each other, but you'll need to know when this makes sense.

TIP #3: INVENT FOR TODAY

You should have a present state for your sovereign power because the form of government may have changed in the past – and again in the future. This happens for quite a few reasons, including war, a weak ruler, and economics. A past colors the present both in monuments, buildings, and other architectural items, but also in population attitude, which is something to add to character backstories.

TIP #4: DECIDE WHO LIVES THERE

We should have an idea what percentage of the overall population each of our species/races is. This helps determine how common other languages are and if the culture of other species is an influence. A reason for the inclusion or exclusion can add tension, such as racism or one species preferring a landscape feature (like a forest) and being there despite attempts at eradicating them.

TIP #5: WHAT'S THE WORLD VIEW?

There are many ideas to assign a sovereign power, including freedom (or lack thereof) to perform magic, own property, use water-based vessels and space craft, and technology generally, or how welcoming they are of species and cultures. *Creating Places* has a list to consider.

TIP #6: GOVERNMENT TYPES: AUTHORITATIVE STATES

Whether an autocracy, totalitarian, dictatorship, or authoritarian government, authoritative states are not the most pleasant ones to live in unless you're the ones in power. With severe restrictions on freedoms, our hero can find himself/herself under duress to accomplish what they desire. They make great places for your hero to destroy or at least kill the state's leader. The differences discussed in *Creating Places* can help make our sovereign powers stand out from each other.

TIP #7: GOVERNMENT TYPES: DEMOCRACIES

A democracy allows people to participate in government by having influence over which policies are made into laws. This means more freedom for the population and therefore our heroes, who might originate from such a place and be philosophically opposed to more oppressive regimes. Wanting to free someone they love or respect from such place can make them heroic.

TIP #8: GOVERNMENT TYPES: FEDERATIONS

Whether an empire, confederation, or unitary state, federations contain states that have some sovereignty over their own affairs while still following the laws of the federation. Some are members voluntarily while others are not, and some can leave when they want but others cannot. Their point of origin is also different.

TIP #9: GOVERNMENT TYPES: MONARCHIES

Kingdoms are common in fantasy but less so in science fiction, but either way, they're not all the same. The two main types are absolute vs. constitutional. The former has a ruler who has no limits on his power—a scenario ripe for abuse, especially with the "divine right of kings" being employed. A constitutional monarchy gives more power to the people via parliament and results in a ruler with often severe restrictions on their powers.

TIP #10: GOVERNMENT TYPES: OLIGARCHIES AND MORE

An oligarchy is any form of government where power is controlled by a small group of people. This could be those in the military, those with magic power, the wealthy, merchants, or other groups we invent. Some of these variations have names like theocracy, aristocracy, or military junta, and each may have stark differences that let us create more variation on our world.

SUMMARY OF CHAPTER 5—SOVEREIGN POWERS

Kingdoms, empires, dictatorships and more are types of sovereign powers that world builders can create. Before we do, a high-level understanding of the differences between them is crucial. Many variations to government types exist, which gives us freedom to tweak details for our needs, but we should know the rules before we break them. The role of sovereignty, including how it is gained and lost, is examined in this chapter along with the "divine right of kings." We also look at the head of state and head of government roles, the differences between them, and the conflicts that can arise. The nature of each branch of government is examined along with parliamentary systems. Democracies, federations, theocracies, monarchies, autocracies and more are examined for their differences.

Inventing a sovereign power should include friends and enemies who shape policy, lifestyle, and culture. The form of government has significant impact on inhabitants and results from world view. History affects this as well, and while creating a history is optional, it enriches the dynamics of relationships and can create heroes, villains, and attitudes in the population. We should consider which species are present and in what percentage, and what languages are spoken or forbidden. Our power's location and climate will impact lifestyles and vegetation, which also influences what natural resources it has or lacks, and what the power does as a result. These can all lead to tensions both with outside powers or the residents within. Symbols, colors, flags, and slogans will be a source of pride and even fear for both foreigners and the population.

SETTLEMENTS

These tips come from Chapter 6 of *Creating Places*.

TIP #1: DO QUARTERS EXIST?

In New Orleans, we have the French Quarter. We can do the same with our species, resulting in an Elven or Dwarven Quarter. We should decide if these exist based on population density; there should be sufficient numbers of a race to do this but not so many that they overflow and live where they please. Decide how accommodating they are of other species entering or staying in their quarter, and how much that quarter caters to their needs.

TIP #2: WHO LIVES HERE?

It's easy to make a settlement mostly human by default, but strive to include other species in prominent ways. Are joint settlements likely at some point, at least somewhere on your world, like the melting pot of America and other parts of the world? Decide where this takes place and what sort of tensions and prejudices creep into daily life. This makes our species seem less like islands.

TIP #3: WHERE IS OLD TOWN?

In large settlements, there's probably an Old Town, which might be called something else, from when the place was first settled. Decide where this is and whether it's a run-down warren of thieves and back alleys or a highly preserved source of pride. Either way, it's likely near the original water source and has smaller streets and shops.

TIP #4: WHAT'S THE TERRAIN LIKE?

Both in and around a settlement, terrain can affect placement and layout of structures, from walls to buildings. Few places are uniformly flat, so where is the higher ground? Did the wealthy stake it for themselves? There might be giant boulders and other obstacles that must be built around. Maybe a wetland encroaches on the town so that some of it is built on stilts, like Venice.

TIP #5: WHAT'S THE CLIMATE?

Climate affects the way people dress and behave. If it's hot and humid, maybe people only work during the morning and night. If it's frigid, maybe they work during the afternoon heat. Customs and expectations also arise from such things. If you've worked out your continent's location, figuring out climate is easy and is almost done for you.

SUMMARY OF CHAPTER 6—SETTLEMENTS

Location impacts a settlement more than world builders realize, from climate to terrain and water supply, but our neighbors also determine how much fortification is needed and the number of armed forces, including their skill sets. Ancient and recent history can bring lasting change and cause attitudes that enrich our setting. Our population's diversity is also critical for determining what life is like for the majority and minorities alike, but first we need to decide who is who (and why), how much power they have, and whether they can subvert those who are supposedly in power. Whether outposts, castles, villages, towns, or cities, or even an orbiting station, a settlement will have secrets, a reputation, colors, symbols, and local lore that characterize it in the minds of inhabitants, friends and enemies.

LAND TRAVEL

These tips come from Chapter 7 of *Creating Places*.

TIP #1: MAKE DRAGONS BELIEVABLE

While anything huge that flies is not believable to start, we can make them more so giving limitations. Even normal birds struggle at high altitudes and might be unable to get over very tall mountains (above 20,000 feet), for example. Dragons and other large animals would never make it unless we decide their magic helps them. We like them all powerful but maybe forcing them to fly around is better.

TIP #2: TERRAIN SLOWS

A forest can slow travelers due to underbrush and being unable to see threats from a distance, requiring caution. Desert sand will stop a wagon and slow walkers, but most deserts are hard earth and just tough on wheels and feet/hooves. Wetlands are worse. Hills and mountains cause fatigue and reduce speed and endurance. However, a road mitigates some of these issues. Be sure to take the terrain into account when determining how long your characters' trip will take.

TIP #3: DON'T DRAW TO SCALE

While it's good to try for accuracy when determining distances and travel times on maps, writing "not drawn to scale" on them gives us leeway to be wrong about something. After all, we're storytellers, not masters at cartography of modes of travel we don't use anymore, like horse, wagon, or hovercraft (I stopped using the latter years ago).

TIP #4: KNOW HOW FAST THINGS TRAVEL

If you're writing fantasy, you need to know how far a horse, wagon, or humans (or a species) moves in a day under normal conditions. Ideally, avoid commenting on it, but this is hard given that characters move through dangerous places and must camp for the night, etc., and we typically mention the dangers while covering said journey. *Creating Places* makes it easier to know this by providing that data.

TIP #5: GET THE TRAVEL TEMPLATE

You can save a ton of time by using the Travel Template sent to newsletter subscribers. It features a way to set the scale on your map, the base distance per day that various animals travel, how to size areas, terrain modifiers, and how long it takes to travel between locations. And if you change your scale, the numbers adjust for you.

Summary of Chapter 7—Travel Over Land

In settings without automobiles, world builders may struggle to determine how long it really takes people to traverse a distance, whether between settlements or land features. Mountains, hills, desert, and vegetation all impact speed and endurance, whether one is walking, riding a steed (even flying on one), or hauling freight. The presence and quality of roads alter this, as do life forms that might cause wariness and therefore slower travel. A methodology is presented to assist with organizing distance measurements and scale, determining the base miles per day (BMPD) for various mode of travel, and terrain modifiers to BMPD. Using both miles and kilometers, formulas are provided for making calculations, which can also be estimated for overall land area in sovereign powers. Newsletter subscribers receive an Excel spreadsheet that can be used to alter scale and modifiers so that all calculations are automatically updated, reducing the need for manual calculations.

Water Travel

These tips come from Chapter 8 of *Creating Places*.

Tip #1: Confusion is Normal

There are many reasons why it's difficult to determine the speed of non-motorized sailing vessels. This includes oarsmen being unable to row continuously, shifting wind speed or direction through a journey, damage to ships, and different degrees of encumbrance (how weighed down it is). All of these change estimates. Maybe it comes as no surprise that we aren't sure how long a trip will take, but *Creating Places* gives you enough info to figure it out.

TIP #2: KNOW YOUR SHIP RATES

Wooden ships are rated based on how many guns and men they have, though the number of decks and masts can imply this as well. In a world without guns, we can still rate them based on armament. Ships of smaller rates were unlikely to attack bigger ships, so take this into account when determining which vessels your story needs.

TIP #3: NO GUNS? NOW WHAT?

In a world without gunpowder, there are no cannons, making our ships tame...unless we find an alternative. Catapults, trebuchets, and ballista all have their pros and cons. The latter could be the best and most effective replacement without causing other believability issues in your work, but you'll need to understand the number of crew needed to operate one vs. a cannon.

TIP #4: KNOW YOUR SHIP TYPES

Whether it's a galley, brig, frigate, galleon, sloop-of-war, or ship-of-the-line, our ship has an appearance, size, capability, and reputation we can utilize with skill. We don't need to invent something new because readers seldom see these and aren't bored with them. We can make changes at will, provided they make sense, because many variations exist on Earth anyway. Feel free to tweak the design of a known vessel...once you know where to start.

TIP #5: DETERMINE BASE SPEEDS FIRST

Most wooden ships average between 2-6 knots over a long trip. They can be becalmed (0 knots) or reach tops speeds of 11 knots, but none sustain that without magic. We can fudge the time needed, but we should know what's possible. This includes being able to convert miles to nautical miles (multiply it by 1.151) and then divide the nautical miles by the average knots to learn how many hours the trip would take.

SUMMARY OF CHAPTER 8—TRAVEL BY WATER

Landlubbers have difficulty determining how long it takes for any ship, whether powered by oars or sails, to traverse a distance. This chapter explores the factors affecting sailing speeds and what vessels are most likely to be used during an Age of Sail period. Calculations are provided for realistic estimates. Both long and round ships are discussed, including the galley, brig, frigate, galleon, sloop-of-war, and ship-of-the-line. In fantasy, we have species and warrior types who might be part of our crew. We might also rule out gunpowder and cannon, which means having ships with no real fire power or which use alternative weapons. Subscribers to *The Art of World Building* newsletter receive an Excel spreadsheet that performs calculations in kilometers, miles, and nautical miles.

SPACE TRAVEL

These tips come from Chapter 9 of *Creating Places*.

TIP #1: "DISTANCE CHANGES"

Remember that everything in space is orbiting something else, and at different speeds, and therefore the distance between two objects is ever-changing. Two planets could be on the same side of the sun at one point in the year but on opposite sides at another. This gives us leeway to decide how long a trip between them would take at a given moment in our story.

TIP #2: "KNOW YOUR ENGINE TYPES"

Our ship might need air breathing engines if it's going to enter an atmosphere, and those are typically rear-facing even if located on the side or elsewhere. Space engines are either jump, hyper, or warp drives, all being public domain options we can use. Each has expected properties and effects, such as time-dilation. Including all three in your story world gives you the most options.

TIP #3: BE CONSISTENT

With invented technologies, try to be consistent with the level of tech people have. A *Star Trek* teleporter and food replicator are equally unbelievable. Would it make sense to have a teleporter but no artificial gravity? Probably not,

because the latter is easier to achieve with a ship that rotates. It would be a mistake to do something like have a
flame thrower but not have open-flame stoves.

TIP #4: DECIDE ON INTERNAL STRUCTURE

Unless your ship has only one room, you should map out
where important rooms are, like the bridge, propulsion,
and crew quarters. This lets you plan how long it takes for
people to move about the ship. The larger the vessel, the
more useful this planning becomes; damage or an intrusion
in one area might mean a lot of time could pass before your
heroes arrive to deal with it. You could do this to avoid
everything being too convenient for them.

TIP #5: DOES YOUR EXTERNAL STRUCTURE MATTER?

Aerodynamics don't matter in space. We've seen and accepted Borg cubes in *Star Trek*. Just decide that your ship
isn't planning to enter an atmosphere before going this
route. Be aware that there is still a stellar wind, but most
readers won't be thinking about this sort of thing.

SUMMARY OF CHAPTER 9—TRAVEL IN SPACE

Science fiction features invented technologies for traveling
the cosmos, but that doesn't free us from attempts to be
realistic about life in space or how to maneuver. Modern
engines operate on the principle of thrust, which requires
rear-facing engines, and we'll need this for slower-than-

light travel within a solar system. Imaginary propulsions, like warp, hyper, or jump drives can benefit from believable limitations. We should remember that locations in space are ever changing positions so that how long it takes to travel between two points is seldom the same—or convenient for our characters. The need to enter a planet's atmosphere affects the ship structure, but world builders will be most interested in the internal organization and the effect we can make this have on people and story.

TIME AND HISTORY

These tips come from Chapter 10 of *Creating Places.*

TIP #1: CREATE A UNIVERSAL CALENDAR

Each kingdom may have its own calendar, which is fine, but how do we know that year 41 AE in Kingdom X is also year 4560 BI in Kingdom Y? A universal calendar. Create one for your own records even if you never share it with the audience.

TIP #2: WHAT DOES YOUR UNIVERSAL CALENDAR START WITH?

If the world acknowledges that universal calendar, you'll need an event recognized everywhere. On Earth, we use the birth of Christ. Does your world have a religious event, technological event (or alien arrival), or supernatural event of such magnitude? If you do, it's probably part of your story world's consciousness. Invent something you like because you'll end up using it.

Tip #3: Be Smart About Names

Don't call a month something like "Snowtime." It is winter in half the world, but it'll be summer in the other half and this won't make sense. And places near the equator aren't getting snow. Ever.

Tip #4: Be Careful Altering Timeframes

We can change the number of minutes in an hour, or hours in a day, but this is unwise because it messes with the audience's sense of passing time. But changing the numbers of days in a week, weeks in a month, or months in a year it has less impact, particularly if we're only off by one. Don't be too extreme unless you really need that for your story. People will forget about your different time frame, or you'll have to remind them all the time. Neither is good.

Tip #5: Create Past Events

There are many events we can put in the past to give spice to the present. Tech events like the first time something happened are appropriate for SF, like ship launches, weapons usage, or drive experiments or failures. Disasters are good, too, even in fantasy worlds, where spells must go wrong sooner or later, sometimes on a huge scale. The gods might do something everyone remembers, too. On the more mundane level are the rise and fall of sovereign powers, wars, groups forming, missions being undertaken, and artifacts being discovered, invented, destroyed, or seemingly lost, the more legendary the better. We can even end up with story ideas from these.

SUMMARY OF CHAPTER 10—TIME AND HISTORY

History can enrich a world and provide us with cultural clashes, famous items, and world figures to which our stories and characters can refer or cite as inspiration. To save time, we can create a master history file with short entries that are invented in a few minutes and which do not need long explanations. Some could be turned into stand-alone stories if we stumble upon a great idea. Historic entries can be created at any time and can include events involving the gods, technology, supernatural, wars, the rise and fall of sovereign powers, artifacts, and famous missions by groups or individuals.

We also need a universal way to measure time because each sovereign power might have its own calendar, making the correlation of events across kingdoms harder. The merits of keeping timeframes similar to Earth's are discussed; this includes the reasons why minutes and hours benefit from little alteration, while the number of days, weeks, and months can experience greater variation without disrupting the audience's sense of time.

PLACES OF INTEREST

These tips come from Chapter 11 of *Creating Places*.

TIP #1: WHAT LIVES IN THE CATACOMBS?

If we create catacombs, decide if monsters, animals, or other creatures live there. Do the surface dwellers know of those inhabitants or the passages? Do they use them, too? What gets hidden here? Try to be creative about your use of these and make it important to your story because just about everything has already been done. We just need a believable reason for their existence, abandonment, and current usage.

TIP #2: USE STEP WELLS

Google "step wells in India" and you'll see some interesting images we can leverage if we have water dwelling species. These could connect to underground rivers and allow for interesting escapes or arrivals. Are they guarded? Are some of these made by the water-dwelling species or by others hoping to reach them?

TIP #3: CREATE PHENOMENON SITES

Places where an accident happened are good for magical, supernatural or technological sites of importance, especially dangerous sites. Just imagine what could go wrong and choose a location and result. These can be good for creating monsters, too, if there's radiation or something similar still going on there. We don't even need good explanations, making this fun to do.

TIP #4: WHAT'S UNDER WATER?

A settlement under the waves offers chances to be innovative. A water-dwelling species makes this more attractive. Shipwrecks (including fallen spacecraft) can also harbor treasure or items that need to be recovered, and which can fall into the wrong hands. They could spawn monsters, too.

TIP #5: THE ORDINARY CAN BE FAMOUS, TOO

Sites of wars, religious incidents, and prophets or martyrs making themselves famous can also acquire significance. Use these places inside settlements or nearby because these can be less dramatic, with no radiation or other residue left over. Not everywhere has to be amazing.

SUMMARY OF CHAPTER 11—PLACES OF INTEREST

Even ordinary locations can acquire significance due to scale, features, or people associated with them. These include monuments, graves, catacombs and hidden passages, and unusual buildings, whether built in stone, flying in the air, or floating on water like Venice. Ruins offer places for treasure to be found or horrors unleashed, including magical or technological items. Event sites and shipwrecks also give inhabitants places to reference, seek, or avoid, and can be where items of our invention originated.

DRAWING MAPS

These tips come from Bonus Chapter 12 of *Creating Places*.

TIP #1: YOU DON'T NEED DRAWING SKILL

With modern map making programs like Campaign Cartographer, you don't need drawing skills to create maps. I can't draw to save my life and have made maps I publish with my works, including *Creating Places*. You just place pre-existing icons for trees, mountains, and settlements and can rearrange them. It takes some imagination but quickly becomes fun to do.

TIP #2: MAPS HELP US INVENT CONFLICT

As we draw land features and seas, we can imagine conflicts between kingdoms about who has access to something and who doesn't, then what they must do to form agreements – or go to war with each other over it. Even if we don't want to write about such things, the sovereign powers where our characters originate are engaged in these conflicts or friendships and our characters will have attitudes based on this.

TIP #3: USE EARTH ANALOGUES

If you have no idea what to draw, just steal somewhere on Earth and purposely do a poor job of drawing the country outline. You can include all the same land features and few will recognize it. You could draw the US with a different shape and then cut it in half, too, or add a sea in the middle. A major change like that makes it less recognizable.

TIP #4: BE SMART ABOUT REGIONAL MAPS

Even if you only want to draw a map of a region, not the whole continent, think about the continent anyway. Things like mountain ranges, prevailing winds, and rain shadows will still affect your region. You needn't draw them; just make a note to yourself that the wind is from "that way" and there's a mountain range "over there."

TIP #5: NO ONE EXPECTS A SETTLEMENT MAP

It can be fun to use City Designer (from ProFantasy) to create city maps, but no one's expecting one in your books. It is worthwhile if the layout is very specific and hard to describe succinctly to an audience, in which case they'll appreciate a map. Only do this if you feel the need to lay out a place, which can be only filled in with the most important buildings you desire.

SUMMARY OF BONUS CHAPTER 12— DRAWING MAPS

While drawing maps is optional in world building, they can help us visualize where everything's taking place, and if done well, can even be included in published works. Drawing skill isn't really needed, as modern map making programs allow us to place pre-existing shapes onto a map and move them around. Continent maps help us decide on the location and qualities of land features like mountains, forests, and deserts so that we create a realistic ecosystem. The location of settlements, rivers, and bodies of water will also impact the stories and lives of characters we create. We can also draw settlement, dungeon, and ship maps to solidify our decisions and find new inspiration in our layouts.

CHAPTER THREE

CULTURES & BEYOND TIPS

Everything not covered in the first two volumes lies within the finale, *Cultures and Beyond (The Art of World Building, #3)*. This includes creating culture, organizations, armed forces, religions, the supernatural, magic systems, technological and supernatural items, languages, names, and various systems our world will have, from health, educational, legal, commerce, to information systems. Finally, we look at how to manage our world building projects. Without these subjects, no world building project is complete.

The tips in this section are from *Cultures and Beyond (The Art of World Building, #3)*.

CULTURES

These tips come from Chapter 1 of *Cultures and Beyond*.

TIP #1: CULTURE CLASH IS USEFUL

Invent culture to cause conflict. Any time we need characters to have bad feelings towards each other, a culture clash is an easy way to create this. For traveling characters, it's a virtual given. People are sensitive and judgmental. We don't need people to have screwed up in a serious way, just offend someone in a trivial one.

TIP #2: UNDERSTAND CULTURAL ORIGINS

Values, beliefs, and morals are the origins of culture. These are ideas. And they manifest as rituals, habits, customs, art, music, and the use of language. We should therefore create those values, beliefs, and morals and then figure out how they manifest (that's culture!).

TIP #3: CONSIDER THE GOVERNMENT

A sovereign power's government greatly impacts culture from the "top down." Consider how much freedom and control people have. Less means less variation at regional, settlement, and social group levels of culture. More freedom means more variation.

TIP #4: KNOW WHAT'S VALUED

While morals and values are slightly different, they can both be used to invent culture. A more high-minded socie-ty will value different traits (like dignity, equality, politeness, and tolerance) than a barbaric one, which might value self-reliance, courage, respect, and integrity.

TIP #5: DETERMINE CULTURAL SCOPE

Are we creating culture throughout a kingdom, region, or social group? Culture trickles down, so what's valued in the U.S. might be less valued on the East Coast, and more valued in New York City, especially in the punk rock scene. Determine what level we're inventing culture for because it's not uniform across all these levels.

TIP #6: DETERMINE CULTURAL VISION

Have an overall vision so that we avoid creating manifestations of culture that clash with each other. An obvious example is elves acting refined at dinner but acting like savages when making love. Invent a vision (which springs from values) that guides our invention of culture, so incongruity doesn't spring up unless we want it to.

TIP #7: RACE AS CULTURE

A frequent complaint is when a fictitious race has a monoculture – every society in that race is identical. The difficulty of creating cultures likely causes this oversight. Don't make all elves the same regardless of where they live or the social class to which they belong. It's not realistic – and yes, people do complain about it.

TIP #8: CREATE CULTURE YOU CAN USE

Some aspects of culture are more useful and should be our focus. This includes greetings, meal etiquette, phrases, rituals, and daily life routines. Other items like songs, clothing, and architecture styles are less helpful because readers won't see them (less true in visual mediums).

TIP #9: ALTER EARTH EXPRESSIONS

We can leverage anything from Earth, but changing our expressions is a quick way to make people seem like they're from somewhere else. "What the hell" becomes "What in Tartarus" for example. Make a list of things you say and just invent alternate versions. It doesn't take long, and the cumulative effect works.

TIP #10: ALTER DAILY ROUTINES

Creating a daily life schedule that differs from Earth is a fast way to make a place seem different. Be sure to use climate as part of this. People in cold places may venture out in midday when it's warmest, while those in hot/humid places might say indoors for a siesta. Having a sense of location helps with regional variations on culture.

SUMMARY OF CHAPTER 1—CREATING CULTURES

This chapter discusses the differences between a culture and a custom, and that morals, values, and beliefs underlie cultural aspects. A cultural vision should be based on these and inform all decisions subsequently made. World builders can determine the scope of an invented culture, as some are regional, or throughout a sovereign power. Cultural depictions have visible, audible, and performance aspects that can be defined. These include body issues such as body language, hair styles, gestures, clothing, and more. Greetings and farewells should be defined because characters will use them. Similarly, swear words, slang, expressions, and colloquialisms can be created to characterize interactions. The daily life of a culture is depicted in dining, bathing, sleeping, employment, and transportation rituals and behaviors, while pastimes, holidays and more create a respite. Even architecture can be influenced.

ORGANIZATIONS

These tips come from Chapter 2 of *Cultures and Beyond*.

TIP #1: WHAT DO THEY WANT?

Every group wants something, so decide whether they want to control an object, possess land, hold power, uphold philosophical ideas, or something else. Not knowing what they want and why makes them unconvincing. We also don't understand what will drive them, upset them, or make them go too far when thwarted. A goal is everything.

TIP #2: DECIDE WHO THEIR
FRIENDS AND ENEMIES ARE

It's too simplistic to decide an organization operates without allies and enemies. Whether individuals, species, kingdoms, or other groups, those connections decide who they are. We sometimes must create those other groups first, but circle back and finish the connection. It will pay off.

TIP #3: CREATE A POWER STRUCTURE

Does power rest with a committee or a single strong man? Is that strength physical or supernatural? Knowing who's really in power and why helps us create tension within the group. Otherwise, they seem to just get along with each other too well. Tension is a story's lifeblood, so don't overlook threats to those in power and how it can taken away, and by who.

TIP #4: HOW DO PEOPLE JOIN OR LEAVE?

Can people leave this group or are they murdered for trying? What do they lose if leaving? How do they join? What must they do to be accepted or remain? This can add tension for members, who may be tempted away by other characters in our story.

TIP #5: CREATE A HISTORY

An organization has people with a shared viewpoint, so what events caused them to band together? What ideas drive people to them? This can be the rise or fall of an idea or government that they miss or want to oppose. Leverage other historical events already in the setting, by creating a group (or two) who dislikes what's happened.

SUMMARY OF CHAPTER 2— CREATING ORGANIZATIONS

Organizations for good or evil are a staple of both fantasy and SF. This chapter discusses both group types and their world views, plus common traits like goals, enemies, friends, and their source of (and quest for) power. How members join and leave such groups is an important element, as some organizations might prevent or inhibit departure. Prerequisites can also bind a member to the group. The history and actions of a group are an important part of its reputation.

ARMED FORCES

These tips come from Chapter 3 of *Cultures and Beyond*.

TIP #1: "WHAT GOVERNMENT TYPE DO THEY WORK FOR?"

Virtually all armed forces groups work for a government, so determine this first. A democracy and a dictatorship will have different armies, for example. How? The latter will be extremely rigid, far more so than the other, including potentially no personal life at all. The military isn't known for great freedom even in a democracy, but imagine how much worse it is in a totalitarian government.

TIP #2: CREATE SYMBOLS AND COLORS

In the real world, we immediately recognize the symbols of the military and make judgments about anything emblazoned with them, from personnel uniforms to buildings and ships. Not creating these is unrealistic, while creating them takes only a minute.

TIP #3: DECIDE HOW PEOPLE JOIN

Knowing what it takes to become a member helps us decide on skills or how elite a group is. This also creates a reputation for members. Are there prerequisites, like the ability to ride a horse or fly a ship? Are certain races forbidden/prized? What physical traits does one need? Can one acquire missing ones like improving strength? What sorts of tests must be passed and how many chances does one get? This adds pressure and pride/humiliation for those trying to join.

TIP #4: UNDERSTAND AND USE EXISTING RANKS

Know what a lieutenant, major, and colonel is in the army and their respective navy or air force counterparts, then use the same ranks and job functions, even if you change the titles for your world, which isn't recommended. Only those in the military usually know these things and aren't bored with them. Confusion (or exposition) is the only result of being clever here.

TIP #5: WHAT'S THEIR REPUTATION?

We all think certain things of each military group in our sovereign power, and so do our characters of theirs, so decide what the group is known for. Are they respected? Feared? Do you pick a fight with one or avoid that? Are you impressed or scornful? This matters even when our characters are not from such a group, because they'll often have to deal with those who are.

SUMMARY OF CHAPTER 3— CREATING ARMED FORCES

Military groups like the army, navy, air/space force, and knights are a staple of both fantasy and SF. We can leverage existing ideas or craft our own. Doing so means deciding how someone joins and leaves a military group, including requirements, tests, and training. Some species and races might be forbidden or assigned special roles, and throughout history, famous members can inspire pride or loathing we can use. When devising military units and ranks, it helps to understand Earth analogues, so some basics are included in this chapter. The world view, uses, locations, place in society, and symbols are all important elements of memorable armed forces and this chapters covers them all.

RELIGIONS

These tips come from Chapter 4 of *Cultures and Beyond*.

TIP #1: START WITH HISTORY

Religions are more tied to history than anything in world building. Invent a prophet and his story which can give us artifacts, holidays, traditions, and more. Virtually everything springs from this, making it the starting point.

TIP #2: THE CONTROL FACTOR

Religions exercise control over practitioner's lives to one degree or another, from how often to pray, when, where, and what words to say, even what actions to perform before, during, and after. These manifestations of faith are critical to how believers and non-believers view the religion. Is it too strict? Not strict enough?

TIP #3: CREATE SYMBOLS

What's a religion without symbols? We create these using our prophet's story. If he first spoke to a god while wearing a cloak, eating an apple, and standing beside a tree type, we have three symbols right there. It's that easy to create them because we're just associating trivial things with momentous occasions.

TIP #4: INVENT CLERGY

Priests can be viewed in specific ways depending on how they act or restrictions that are placed on them. This reflects on an entire religion and how the populace view it. Are there scandals that affect them, or do they fear that one will emerge? Power is held by those in high regard, so how can the clergy fall from grace based on inappropriate behavior by wayward members? What defines "wayward?"

TIP #5: DO THEY CONVERT?

Are there missionaries in this religion or do they let people come to them? The former is significant because it makes them active, rather than passive, characters who might upset people, including our characters, whom they try to convert. The religion will have a reputation for this if so. Use it to personalize them.

Summary of Chapter 4—Creating Religions

While some items we create have history as a minor element, history is crucial with religions, so first we look at where and how the religion formed, including a prophetic figure and the role of a god, should one exist. Creation and end of world myths, and the afterlife, are important elements that potential followers consider, along with the requirements for worship and the penalty for failing to follow the rules. How someone joins and leaves a religion can be trivial or significant and includes the possibility of expulsion. We'll need holy sites, too, and a decision on holidays, languages, customs, sects, relationships with everyone from species to other religions, and what members of the clergy are like and their role in society. Most importantly, we need the symbols and beliefs of this religion.

The Supernatural

These tips come from Chapter 5 of *Cultures and Beyond*.

Tip #1: Origins Aren't Needed

Even scientists sometimes don't understand where various energies they've detected originate, so we don't need to state this either. That said, an interesting idea that creates even more mystery is never a bad thing. In fantasy, there's a tendency to decide the gods did it, so SF seems to offer more opportunity for mystery.

TIP #2: DETERMINE PREVALENCE

How often is a phenomenon encountered? It may always exist but only flare up at certain times, maybe even regularly, like the "Old Faithful" geyser. Or supernatural elements might be common, which tends to reduce reactions to them. Decide how often the event occurs and whether rarity is something the story needs.

TIP #3: DETERMINE IMPACT

If the supernatural is very common, such as everyone being able to cast minor spells, then this could greatly impact society. Unless we intend to think our way through every detail, it's sensible to decide that magic, for example, is quite limited, as is often shown in fantasy. Thinking our way through every detail can lead to many unique revelations which set our world apart.

TIP #4: DO SUPERNATURAL CREATURES EXIST?

If so, they often take the form of extensions to their abilities, such as a horse that runs faster or can cross into other realities. Decide what problems the story has and how something like this can help, but be careful not to make the solution perfect. For example, make the faster horse unable to go all the way to their destination.

TIP #5: ARE THERE DEMI-GODS?

A figure like Cupid is a lesser god with a specific function. We can create such individuals if we need them, or if they can affect our characters' lives. We can also create half-gods like Hercules. Decide on their abilities, origins, function, and reputation. A few infamous past deeds round them out.

SUMMARY OF CHAPTER 5— CREATING THE SUPERNATURAL

Supernatural elements exist in both fantasy and SF and can be used to add to the unexpected. The audience may expect magic, for example, but not our version of it, so there's room for originality here. We can also create energies that give rise to phenomena, beings, or places like magic pathways or alternate worlds and realities that impact our setting and stories. How much impact and prevalence these supernatural elements have, and how to determine this, are an important focus of this chapter.

SYSTEMS OF MAGIC

These tips come from Chapter 6 of *Cultures and Beyond*.

TIP #1: ARE UNPREDICTABLE RESULTS POSSIBLE?

In some worlds, like Harry Potter, spells that aren't cast correctly still "go off" but with unexpected results. Is this possible in your setting? Or does the spell fail? The latter seems more believable; the ability to so easily screw it up makes magic so absurdly dangerous that it's likely forbidden pretty much everywhere.

TIP #2: DECIDE IF SPELLS ARE NEEDED

Do people need to recite memorized lines, make gestures, or use physical materials to do magic? Or can they do it by force of will, like a god? In theory, spells are to achieve a specific result within a range of possible results, meaning limits are built in. The caster's skill and strength determine where in the possible range their spell falls. But if willing things to happen, there may be fewer limits and more inherent danger. What makes sense for the story?

TIP #3: HAVE A GOOD NAME

While we can just call it "magic" and keep it simple, this doesn't work when there's more than one type in the setting. Invent cool names for each to increase audience attraction. We can also call the practitioners a related name instead of the generic "wizard," for example. This distinguishes our setting, too.

TIP #4: SANDERSON'S LAWS ARE NOT LAWS

Author Brandon Sanderson proposed three "laws" of magic systems that are not laws but guidelines that should not make us feel restricted, but they're worth noting. They amount to making the reader understand the magic before using it to solve problems, creating limitations on magic, and expanding what you have before adding new ideas. Sound advice!

TIP #5: DECIDE WHAT TRAINING IS NEEDED

What can magic users do without training? Anything at all? Do they need formal training to become powerful, skilled, or even be allowed to perform magic? Refusal to accept training is an easy way to make someone an outlaw. Decide what sort of training is available and from who (person, group, guild, university, sovereign power). Defining this allows us to create distinctions between wizards who received training from one or another.

SUMMARY OF CHAPTER 6— CREATING A SYSTEM OF MAGIC

Magic systems can be simple or complex, but they should always be consistent. This chapter discusses the methods and principles of good systems and how to create them. This includes the importance of naming them, deciding if spells are needed and what those are for, whether spells can go wrong and how, and different types of magic we might want to include in our settings. We'll also look at how much training someone might need, what forms that training takes, and learn how to decide what's right for our setting. And no discussion of magic is complete without a look at how to invent spells.

ITEMS

These tips come from Chapter 7 of *Cultures and Beyond.*

TIP #1: USE STANDARD FORMS

Don't be afraid to create magic items that are typical in form, like jewelry or clothes. Being able to wear the item minimizes the risk of loss and keeps it handy when it's suddenly needed. This is a huge advantage, so while a magic ring is a cliché, that form of item is also helpful.

TIP #2: LIMIT THEIR POWERS

For both tech and magic items, make sure they don't solve a character's problems perfectly or it's too convenient. Something must go wrong. The battery in a tech item might have drained. A magic item can suffer a similar fate, a rationale being that whoever created the spell wasn't powerful enough to make it better.

TIP #3: AVOID TALKING ITEMS

The infamous talking sword is a fast way to get mocked, and yet we have devices that talk to us now, not to mention AI in SF, where we can get away with it. But in fantasy, it's still frowned upon without a good explanation.

Tip #4: Marry Form to Function

The purpose of an item doesn't always match its form. The powers in magic rings, wands, and staves have little to do with their shape. This is often true of tech, too. When the purpose is more active, marry function to form, such as an arrow or sword designed to strike something.

Tip #5: Invent Regular Items, Too

Everyday items acquire significance by being associated with famous (or infamous) people and events, like a prophet, hero, villain, or royalty. We and our characters are less likely to make a big deal of these, but creating them fleshes out our setting. Besides, making a big deal out of everything is like having high drama every moment.

Summary of Chapter 7—Creating Items

Whether magical, technological, or more ordinary, memorable items exist in our setting even if we don't mention them. SF likely expects them, and fantasy often has at least one magic item someone has or covets in a story, but even ordinary items can be given significance through association with important people, places, or events. This chapter discusses how to invent their properties, origins, and form, and how to determine who is likely to use or want them. The creation of an A.I. is included.

LANGUAGES

These tips come from Chapter 8 of *Cultures and Beyond*.

TIP #1: READ BOOKS

There are several books on how to create languages, including *The Art of Language Invention* by the guy who created Dothraki for *Game of Thrones*. Reading this will convince you this is doable or not – and what you need to know if doing yourself or even hiring someone else.

TIP #2: THEY CAN BE A DISTRACTION

No one but us understands these words and they can distract a reader. Even those who take the time to sound them out have been pulled out of our story while they do so. We may want to just avoid this altogether.

TIP #3: WE HAVE THREE OPTIONS

We can ignore language creation, we can make up nonsense words as we go along, or we can create a real language to one degree or another. The only people who'll really know which we did are conlangers, a small group of people whose opinion might not matter to us!

TIP #4: YOU MAY COACH A NARRATOR

If you hire someone to create an audiobook for you, you'll need to coach them on how to say everything unless you do the book yourself. Make sure you can say everything yourself if this might happen.

TIP #5: HIRE A PRO

The Language Creation Society's (LCS) site at https://conlang.org/ makes it easy to hire an expert for as little as $100 US or up to $800. The difference is how much they give you. But understanding what we're getting may require reading those books I mentioned.

SUMMARY OF CHAPTER 8— CREATING LANGUAGES

Creating a language is one of the most challenging aspects of world building, but it's also one of the few that we can outsource; how and where to do so is discussed. Even so, some basic terms must be understood so we know what we're buying and receiving from our expert. If we choose to do it ourselves, we should consider whether it benefits our audience and how, or whether it's even a burden that we can save both them and ourselves. This chapter will not teach world builders how to invent a language because there are entire books on the subject, and those are referenced here, but it will discuss the pros and cons of constructing a language and what we lose by not having one (or more).

NAMES

These tips come from Chapter 9 of *Cultures and Beyond.*

TIP #1: AVOID APOSTROPHES AND HYPHENS

The use of both is cliched. If doing this, make sure most names from that culture are the same so it doesn't seem like we're just trying to be exotic, which is how this got a bad reputation. The hyphens are caused by concatenating a mother and father's surname. An apostrophe replaces missing letters and we can easily live without doing that.

TIP #2: KEEP NAMES SHORT

Long names are a way to distinguish one race from another, but no one likes trying to sound out Limineraslyvarisnia, for example. However, such names can exist, so if we do this, only use that long version once and shorten it for the rest of the book, such to "Limi."

TIP #3: ALTER EXISTING WORDS

We can take words we see around us and remove or replace letters and syllables to make new words. We can add prefixes or suffixes. We can substitute vowels. These techniques are fun and effective.

Tip #4: Surnames Sources

We can use places, occupations, nicknames, and first names for "last" or surnames. This helps us reuse places and names we've already created. Places can imply a character's origins, but some, like "Hill," are too generic for that. Professions can imply at least their parent's background, such a blacksmith getting the last name "Smith."

Tip #5: Avoid Name Generators

There are free online programs that can create names for us with a button click. A quick search will turn them up. But they tend to feel impersonal and when we need multiple names, these programs are unlikely to create ones that seem to fit together.

Summary of Chapter 9—Creating Names

Many techniques exist for creating names of people, places, and things, and all of them leverage our creativity to make the results and process more satisfying than using name generators, which are also discussed. Caveats and pitfalls abound, for while a great name elevates our story, bad ones turn off audiences, or keep them from talking about a character with an unpronounceable or unspellable name. We look at the differences between given names, surnames, compound names, and different ways to leverage parts of our invented world for all of them. The tips in this chapter will make this required activity fun and rewarding.

OTHER SYSTEMS

These tips come from Chapter 10 of *Cultures and Beyond.*

TIP #1: SIMPLIFY MONETARY SYSTEMS

Audiences don't care about our monetary system or want to remember it. We'll seldom be mentioning it anyway. In the U.S. we just say "dollars" and "cents," never mentioning pennies, nickels, etc., so do the same in a fictional world. It can even be smart to say that an $100 item here is a 100 credit item in SF, for example. Why figure out what everything is worth?

TIP #2: INVENT SOME CRIMES

In a world with magic or new tech, we have crimes unknown to Earth. This is a fun imagination exercise, including deciding punishments. Be reasonable about why the laws exist and find ways characters can be constrained by or run afoul of them. This is likely when traveling.

TIP #3: KNOW YOUR UNITS

In commerce, units of weight mean the amount of gold, for example, determines the value. But units of value mean the item has no value beyond what's printed on it, like paper money; the paper itself is worthless. Units of value become worthless when the government backing them collapses and may not be present in fantasy settings as a result.

TIP #4: HOW EDUCATED IS EVERYONE?

In fantasy settings, educational levels tend to be lower, as in the 1500-1700s on Earth, while SF often suggests people are more educated, but they needn't be. Ignorant people can drive a car well, and maybe they can fly a spaceship, too, especially if it has an A.I. they just need to command. Either way, should work out how much education is expected and whether characters met that or not.

TIP #5: HOW INFORMED IS EVERYONE?

Regardless of education, information flow can be compromised. In fantasy, it's typically word of mouth and prone to some inaccuracy. In SF, it might be better, but that's assuming people have access to data; they may not, and for our story needs we can choose how ignorant they are. This helps us create biases that place them at odds with those who bring more info, creating conflict. This is a good reason to restrict information flow in both genres.

SUMMARY OF CHAPTER 10—OTHER SYSTEMS

Other systems exist in our setting and warrant development. We'll examine educational systems and their impact on employment, plus where and how people are getting educated or being disqualified from it. Health systems include medical and mental, and they range from great to terrible, each having significant impacts on lives. Information systems aren't just for SF, because fantasy settings need to disseminate information, too, and have their own ways of doing so. Understanding monetary systems and how to keep them simple is another focus and includes how to determine the value of time, labor, and materials. And no world is complete without laws, crimes, and punishments, so developing a legal system is a critical world building task we breakdown into a manageable one.

CONCLUSION

These tips come from Chapter 11 of *Cultures and Beyond.*

TIP #1: STAY ORGANIZED

However you do it, keep your world building files organized so that you can easily find information. And don't repeat info in more than one place because you won't remember to change it in both. I keep a master spreadsheet where I can see, at a glance, certain basics about every city on a continent such as population, races present, age, colors, and symbols. And in each city file, I don't mention these things, alluding to the spreadsheet.

TIP #2: FOLLOW YOUR OWN RULES

If we state that no one can do something, don't have someone be able to do it. The exception is when a character is special in achieving this impossible result, but do that on purpose, not because you made up a rule, forgot, and then had someone break it without even commenting on it. Audiences notice these things. Keep a list of your rules and do yourself a favor – don't be ironclad about them. This gives us flexibility to break one when we need to.

TIP #3: CONSIDER A PARTNER

World building can take huge amounts of time. Consider doing a joint venture with friends where you build a setting together, collaborating and dividing up the work. Just be advised that if this friendship ever fails, you may start arguing over who gets to use the setting. A simple written agreement can specify you each have ownership to write stories in it, but you'll need to work out these details.

TIP #4: REMEMBER TO HAVE FUN

Try not to get so bogged down in world building that it's no fun anymore and you don't have time to write stories – or promote them. Use the resources I've provided to help you decide what to skip and when. World Building University has a free course that's designed to help you decide what to do. Use promo code "185Tips" once "Accelerated World Building" is available!

TIP #5: USE WORLD BUILDING TOOLS

Whether it's my series, *The Art of World Building*, my school World Building University, or books, podcasts, and YouTube videos by others, get familiar with many opinions on how things can be done and take all of it with a grain of salt. There are few things we must get "right." Be flexible and don't get overwhelmed.

SUMMARY OF CHAPTER 11—CONCLUSION

In the series conclusion, we look at how to organize our files of world building notes so that the info glut doesn't become overwhelming; this includes some tools others have created, whether free or not, and the pros and cons of using them. We'll also look at different approaches to world building and how they can affect our working methodology and results. Final thoughts include the merits of following our own rules per world and whether partnering with another world builder is a good idea or not.

About The Author

Randy Ellefson has written fantasy fiction since his teens and is an avid world builder, having spent three decades creating Llurien, which has its own website. He has a Bachelor of Music in classical guitar but has always been more of a rocker, having released several albums and earned endorsements from music companies. He's a professional software developer and runs a consulting firm in the Washington D.C. suburbs. He loves spending time with his son and daughter when not writing, making music, or playing golf.

Connect with me online

http://www.RandyEllefson.com
http://twitter.com/RandyEllefson
http://facebook.com/RandyEllefsonAuthor

If you like this book, please help others enjoy it.

Lend it. Please share this book with others.
Recommend it. Please recommend it to friends, family, reader groups, and discussion boards
Review it. Please review the book at Goodreads and the vendor where you bought it.

JOIN THE RANDY ELLEFSON NEWSLETTER!

Subscribers receive discounts, exclusive bonus scenes, and the latest promotions and updates! A FREE eBook of *The Ever Fiend (Talon Stormbringer)* is immediately sent to new subscribers!

www.ficiton.randyellefson.com/newsletter

RANDY ELLEFSON BOOKS

TALON STORMBRINGER

Talon is a sword-wielding adventurer who has been a thief, pirate, knight, king, and more in his far-ranging life.

The Ever Fiend
The Screaming Moragul

www.fiction.randyellefson.com/talonstormbringer

THE DRAGON GATE SERIES

Four unqualified Earth friends are magically summoned to complete quests on other worlds, unless they break the cycle – or die trying.

The Dragon Gate

www.fiction.randyellefson.com/dragon-gate-series/

THE ART OF WORLD BUILDING

This is a multi-volume guide for authors, screenwriters, gamers, and hobbyists to build more immersive, believable worlds fans will love.

Volume 1: Creating Life
Volume 2: Creating Places
Volume 3: Cultures and Beyond
Volume 4: Creating Life: The Podcast Transcripts

Volume 5: Creating Places: The Podcast Transcripts
Volume 6: Cultures and Beyond: The Podcast Transcripts
185 Tips on World Building
The Complete Art of World Building

Visit www.artofworldbuilding.com for details.

RANDY ELLEFSON
MUSIC

INSTRUMENTAL GUITAR

Randy has released three albums of hard rock/metal instrumentals, one classical guitar album, and an all-acoustic album. Visit http://www.music.randyellefson.com for more information, streaming media, videos, and free mp3s.

2004: The Firebard
2007: Some Things Are Better Left Unsaid
2010: Serenade of Strings
2010: The Lost Art
2013: Now Weaponized!
2014: The Firebard (re-release)

Made in the USA
Middletown, DE
13 May 2020